ASCENSION

SHIRLEY FREEMAN WYNN

DEDICATION

To all who are Templates, dedicated, and with clarity,
doing the work of building the Beloved Community as heaven on earth,
wherein each knows Self as Divine Love.
Thank you for mirroring the promised Christed life.
Keep loving until the day we will all know ourselves as Divine Love.

TABLE OF CONTENTS

I WANT THAT LOVE

I want that love
That love that has no needs
That love sufficient in Itself
That love that knows itself as I Am
That love that is given by Grace
That love that creates and amplifies
That love that blesses all

I want that love
That love that is worthy
That love that knows itself as Divine
That love yours and mine
That love with ego surrendered
That love with the power to heal
That love that creates abundance
That love that enables self and others

I want that love
That love filled with passion and calm
That love that has a shared vision
That love that inspires and creates beauty
That love that is aware of Divine mission
That love that knows and embraces all
That love that lives from the heart
That love where God and self are one

WHEN LOVE COMES

When Love comes
It never looks as expected
It's always too something or other
Not the image of ego choice
It probably will not fit the culture
Highly likely to be misunderstood
Remember you are looking at the packaging
Open and see what heaven brought.

Forgoing judgements required
Rising above cultural conditioning
Closing the eyes of learned behavior
Opening the eye of the soul
The way forward to unblocking
Magical gifts of the Divine
The gift sent to bring you home to Self
To the abundant fruits of the promised heaven
Which looks like a mirage
From the dark night of the soul.

You will not have to say a word
Nor tell what you've found
It will be written on your life
Expressed in your eyes
A life lived from the soul
Reflected in every action.

WHO KNEW

The right love in the wrong time
God's joke or is it that God does not
Use your clock or your calendar?
Amazing love only the soul can know.

An urge to grow in self-love
Available and unlimited to make
Whole and abundant
A love with the gift of unlimited joy
Available to all but not without the work
Of ego surrendered to higher Self
Which enables purpose, meaning, abundance.

Even after being told such a love is available
Who would believe it?
No one before the experience
So say amen, thank you, hallelujah, amen
Then move and live in the spirit of love
Only grace can gift such a blessing.

WE DIDN'T ASK FOR THIS LOVE

How could one ask?
There was no way of
knowing so powerful a love
Is available on this earthly journey.
If it's that one must be the chosen
I say thank you but please show mercy.
Not my will but Thy will be done.

I ask only for guidance and help
As this gift came without instructions
for assembly or manual, triggering
Dark night of my soul in preparation for
Your gifts Divine bringing us closer to
The love that we have within.
Born to be, the Divine manifested on earth.
To share your gifts for earth given at birth.

I see myself as perfect love
In the mirror of your eyes.
The same fire that lights the sun and stars.
I see you I see myself.
I see life lived in love.
It leaves me no choice but to
Become what I see.
Do the work necessary to
Embody perfect love as self love.
Old wounds, hurts, betrayals to cleanse
Forgiveness of self and others required.

Each must enter the cave of ego self
Climb up one's Calgary Hill
Name the scabs that cover the wounds
Clear out the pain and replace with
Forgiveness of self and others
Wear the crown of the glorified
Of a healed and joyfilled human being
Living the Christ model.

THE PEARL

No matter how challenging life becomes
Remember that only
Oysters that have been wounded
Produce pearls
No need to hide your wounds
Cracks left let in the Light Divine
Wear your pearls of love
Grace shelters you now
Ask and it shall be given

The rewards of Re-membering
Self as God essence
Loving the self opening the way
For embracing all
New vision that sees
The Divine in all creation
In full knowledge of no separation

Felt in full when my heart is next to yours
And I re-member fully and
Become wholly love
A vibration requiring nothing
More that the light in your eyes
To know the rapture of Divine love

THE SOUL REMEMBERED

I've found something of great value
That I didn't know I needed and
Could never know how to find.
How and what part of me is so aware
Of what it wants me to become that
It finds ways to put what is needed
For growth in my path?

Something that drops me into the Mystic
That otherworldly place where
Fragments of my soul are remembered
And bought back into daily life
Enriching the Ordinary with Bliss
Peace and Supernatural love.

A source available to all but
Separated by learned rules
Expectations and daily burdens
A gift to enrich Life
In ways gold and things cannot
Awakening the heart and informing
Life with a way of being more
Suited to living in peace, joy, and love.

LOVE'S DEMANDS

Never has love required so much of me
Calls forth nags I thought were healed
Tops went but roots
Intact and riotously growing.
Digging up roots for a healing
The rewards being
Gold found under roots.

Under the influence of a
Love that gives strength
And the feeling of safety
And strength to look
At long-buried wounds
In search of forgiveness
Reconciling and healing.

Broken places and wounds
Entrusted to love
Healed and light entered
Into healed places.
The power of love
To make whole again.

RUN RABIT RUN

You've seen your Self and
It frightened you so much
You thought I was the cause
All you saw was your own love
I am only the mirror

Run, pray, doubt, and swear.
Do what ego knows to do
You'll understand it better by and by.
You'll know yourself
Embrace yourself as love
Thereby knowing then what I know now.

I have a vision of you
As that ego-surrendered Self
Arrayed in the splendor of your divinity
Holding a mirror is all I'm required to do
Seeing then becoming only you can do
Exhausting and confusing
Is the pathless path
Endurance will make you strong and free
Knowing the Divine was in
The lead all the time .

JUST AS I AM

At sea literally and emotionally
Willing to let what is Be what it is
Just look and examine my heart and mind
As they give different perspectives of my life
Mind is saying there is no place in society
For what your heart is telling you
My heart says well that's a pity cause
It's exactly what is sorely missing and needed
And your assignment on this earth is
To make a place a better place
A home for love a home for joy
A home for peace a home for me.

You are a vessel for containing ME
I sent you came in you to be a depository
For my love in the world
You and I are knowing this in heart and mind
There is agreement on something so let's see within
Between what more we can make aligned for peace
What do you want? What feels right
And contains no feeling of doubt?
Embracing with heart and mind the love
We both feel is the best most satisfying
Stand in that and leave the rest to ME
Live my higher power.
Do nothing, be everything.

Standing above it all while it's all within
I worked it out before sending you two
Trust my timing
All I do I do for you
You he and I are One.
That's why you two
Feel the love we share. That is the attraction.
Those are my vibrations. The power of the
Energy to do my work. Claim it and create
Whatever you want. Just think it. Feel it.
Watch it manifest. The work has been
And was done when you embraced love
My first commandment after which life
Is fulfilled alive. Now live!!!!!

LOVE DIVINE

All who are chosen and offered a mighty love
A love requiring a clear vision
Brought to awareness by another
Will require an understanding not readily available
A leveling up to a vibrational level
More Christ-like is required.
A seeing beyond just eyesight.

A period in the belly of the whale
A time away and travel within the self
A self previously denied one's embrace
A death and a rebirth
A heart large enough to embrace all Creation
A love not limited to previous cultural understanding.

Easier to stay with the paint-by-the-numbers life and love
But a Divine gift bestowed cannot be refused
Great gifts require a death of the small self and a rebirth
Embracing the love of the Divine
Then living the love that we are manifesting
The Divine love in living.
Expect nothing to be the same.
You've been changed.

LOVING OURSELVES

When love calls one to self-love
With that look into the eyes of the lover
And sees oneself as love
Pray all the gods come to your aid
As the real work of this life has begun.

We'll say we want to be loved and to love
What we really want is to love ourselves
Challenging with huge efforts
To take that forensic audit of one's history
And reconcile the pain we have caused and
The pain we accepted without challenging.
On some level we knew better.

All the while you know
God is love and now
You are love
Call all the angels to assist
For learning a new way to be
Fully alive in the world.
The work you came here to do
The gifts for the world
Assigned to you at birth
Now manifest into full bloom
You are love and loving.

MAKE SPACE FOR GRACE

We were commanded to love one another
Now that we are lovers
Of life and one another
Let us yield and make space
For Divine Grace.

Trust the promise of the Great Lover
Allow acceptance of The New Thing
We are promised
The price has already been paid.

Be the light the world needs
Wherever you stand on this
Blue green planet our home.
Being the love that you are
Gives permission and example
For others to join in.

OWN YOUR FEAR

Your fear is yours
You created it and must chose to own it
However you have not
Because you ask not
There is another option
Surrender the ego to the I AM
Come into your birthright and purpose
A very frightening option
Surrender the ego to Higher Self.

So I say run, work harder, run faster
When you get there you will still be here.
I've done my work
Mirrored you as the
Divine Love that you are
Born to bring forth gifts for self and others
In fear of that Self you run from
Well, run, work harder, run faster.

Until you choose to embrace Self
A work that comes with a price
An exchange of the ego self for Divine Self
Awaken to who you are
Realize that the promise
Of the miracles of Divine Grace
Covers all and fear cannot live
Where love abides.

SUPPORTED BY LOVE

Floating in the warm sea
Warmed by the sun
Covered in a blanket of blue sky above
Cares washed away
Surrendering to love
Totally provided for in all ways.

Concerned about the wars of all kinds
Being an example of the possibilities
Provided for man
To float in a sea of beauty
In body and in mind
Memories of the promised paradise
Always at hand.

No rewards or value
Can be redeemed from hate
No peace can be the obtained from
Hate so old no one remembers
Why ancestors started the fight
In a time of I AM forgotten.

Let's start anew
Me loving me so I can love you
Only one of us here
Remembering a time
of unity mind
So hold me like the ocean
Then I will disappear
Back in the ecstasy
Original paradise reclaimed.

A LOVE THAT CALLS ME

Love calling me home to Myself
Rooting out old injuries,
False ideas, betrayals, abandonment, and pain
Dark night of the soul work
Love enabling healing
Soul restoration work

What a blessing to get The Call
Better still to answer yes
Do the work that
Enables joy in a world of cares
Where glimpses of heaven
For earthly living are a given
Love of Divine Self the prize

Blessings come with burdens
Preparations for endurance
Steadfastness for the work at hand
The way to make strong
A cross before a crown
Earned not given

THE TIME THAT PASSES
MUCH TOO FAST

The time that passes much too fast
The time that I want to last
The time when looking into your eyes
The time I see myself as Love Divine
The time the meaning I AM is fully known
The time of merging of earth and heaven
The time that says you are home

The time when colors are more vivid
The time when sound is clear
The time when all senses are heightened
The time when life is aware of itself
The time when Life is in perfect order

The time when cares are no more
The time when health is perfect
The time when beauty abounds
The time at home within self
The time when no doubt can find us
The time when we know all is love
The time of the promised heaven
The time all mankind longs for
The time promised to all
The time ego is surrendered to Divine
The time self love is known

A FULL HALLELUJAH

The light I saw in you
My own Divine reflection
And the thrill of welcoming
Myself to myself
Home again Free

No debts owed for freedom bought
Mine all the while
Me myself and I
Just a free exchange
A gift all can afford
What we can do for each other

Amazing Grace
A full hallelujah
And pass the love on
The world awaits
This precious gift

THE TWO VOICES

My mind said stop, let it go.
It's a hopeless situation,
Foolish and without cultural value.
Nothing can be done
To change the situation.

My heart replied,
"Hope is my domain."
My head is filled with false teachings
And other people's doubts,
Mostly about things they were
Taught, not something experienced
From ages long past.

Come with me.
I know a secret door,
A Divinely-sourced door,
Hidden from the view of others
And saved just for you.

Trust your heart.
It listens to the creator
Of such doors.
Enter a dimension filled with
Heart desires saved just for you.

THERE ARE DAYS

There are days I wish I had never seen you
There are more days when I wish
I could see you all day and
Share with you all night.
There are times I think I dreamed you up
Then days I think you were heaven sent
An image of my imagination
Fairy tale and then nightmare
Comfort and torture, both without blame.

Knowing that there is noone here but me
An energetic projection of me onto you
Needing to learn to reclaim
All that is myself without casting doubt.
Strange there is no fear
Just a work to be done until all becomes clear.

Call it love, insanity, or call it ascension
Names mean little here
It's beyond explanation
Its energy ever-changing evolving
To reach Its origin
Where unity abides and love
Knows itself and says I AM.

THIS WORK

Now that I remember who I am
I've come to remind you of who you are.
We are here to fulfill the Divine assignment
Even though that task is yet to be revealed.
Intuitively I know we are well-prepared
To do the work, and I trust
Divine timing completely when
All will be revealed and supported completely

On second thought
Remembering who we are
Actually is the work we are here to do.
Nothing more required
Stand in awe of what is to be revealed
In Divine Timing.

Look and listen attentively to the signs
Subtle though they be
The voice and actions of the Divine
Are not found in the noise of the world
Your heart knows what is for you.

WHAT IS LOVE?

Love is not hugs kisses and sex
Although they can be awesome
The shelf life of satisfaction is limited
And empty without Divine love.
Love is being a mirror reflecting the
God essence of the Beloved. A safe
Space to grow into the vision being shown.

The first time I saw myself as a reflection of God
Within the mirror you held for me
I knew I loved that woman wanted to be her
Had to earn her. Aware that now I have a
Safe birthing place a sacred space to
Bring forth a Divine self.

Self love the beginning and the end
Nothing more to do
A time to be love in all situations.
No matter how things appear
All is well and all will be well
Love Divine has it covered.

WHO ARE YOU?

I thought I was happy
Then you came and mirrored
The truth of love
And I knew that I was living a lie
Fully answering to the matrix
And things were not as they seemed.

So much truth hurts
As it cleans the wounds
Lies half-truths and betrayals
Peeling back falsehoods
A mirror revealing
The pure God essence of
My truth the I AM
I can no longer deny but
Fully embrace and live.

The greatest gift of all
Lifetimes of searching cannot find
Buried within awaiting a mirror to reveal
A pearl of great value
The love of self
Enabling the love of others
Unlimited abundance in all areas
Home at last in the house of self-love

YOUR EYES

The light I see in your eyes
My own Divine reflection
The thrill of welcoming
Myself to myself
A rebirth
Home

No debts owed for freedom bought
Mine all the while
Me, myself, and I
Just a free exchange
A gift all can afford
What we can do for each other

Amazing Grace
A full hallelujah
And pass the love on
The world awaits
This precious gift

BROKEN-HEARTED

Broken places let in the Light of Divine love,
The glue which holds universes in orbit.
It will hold you as well.
Love lost breaks us all.
To begin mending, hold your heart next
To a beloved's heart and get a reset.
Each loving heart holds Divine Essence.

You are not alone in your pain.
Great Love holds you still.
Everything changes after a heartbreak, death of body not soul.
Love is not lost; just a breath away.
A new way of seeing is required.
The pain caused by a lack of bodily presence
Is real; however our true essential spirit
Is ever present with the beloved.
Just a memory away.

Loving deeper and fuller is the lesson in the pain.
Be ever aware and present to the gift of life.
Completely aware of the gift of breath and love.
Move fully into life
Wounded though you be.

ELIXIR OF THE CHESTNUT TREE

Two fishes and three loaves
Fed the multitude because
The elixir, love, is a multiplier
The foundation of prosperity
In multiple dimensions.

Standing under the chestnut tree
Which grows hardily in France
But is extinct in USA
Showing me how much living can be
Packed in a few minutes with the power of
Being fully present and alive
With the elixir of joy in our hearts.

Chestnut tree is called the bread tree,
Known traditionally for its elixirs of
Abundance, provisions, and longevity.
Feed the people generously.
You didn't have a long time to stand
Under the Chestnut tree
As you were called suddenly to your
Home in another dimension.

Joy, being the elixir
Not limited by space and time,
Visits my mind and lives in my heart
Reminding me of the power of love
That keeps giving and bringing me
Pink flowers and new growth and joy
In memories treasured and shared.

ETERNAL

We've loved each other a million times
In thousands of places
That's why this feeling is so familiar
Yet new every time
The memories are so deeply
Placed in every cell and
Available without touch or repeating
Making way for other work to be done
In this time and space.

Every time I see your face
Memories of your touch
Trigger a cellular response
Filled with deepest satisfaction
Bringing me home again to self and
To the love remembered renewed and forever
Satisfying, making the world a paradise
With no distance no matter how far away
We are one from the other,
Whole and divinely held.

EVER CHANGING TIMES

Has the world changed or is it I
Who is no longer recognizable?
Time means nothing.
Space and distance have no meaning.
You are always present
Just because I AM

No need for hello
When goodbye is of no use.
A complete restructuring of reality.
What new language can I use?
The learned language no longer
Describes my reality.
How do I speak to anyone other than you
Who knows how to live
This new reality?

Are we to be a planet of two?
Are there other lovers
Who know this blessed affliction?
Even if no others exist
I will never be lonely or alone.
With your love and mine, I'm safe.
We will be a living example
Of the possibilities.
God's blueprint for joy of living
Available when there is self love.

GOD'S SAVING GRACE

Each time I've almost been defeated
Some one entered my life
To remind me of God's love for me
Reactivating my knowledge of my God self.
Now it's you who have arrived in this dark period of doubt and trouble
With the gift and power of Divine love
Jolting self-remembrance

Sending off electromagnetic vibrations of love hitting
Like solar flares upon earth
Bringing color and light to restore and renew
Enliven and delight
Finding my way home to Self
By the light of love emanating from inside

A gift to savor and share
Create and hold close
In deep gratitude and
With whole hallelujahs
For Grace freely given
Joyfully received and returned
I say I AM

BROKEN PLACES

You couldn't or wouldn't love me
And I thank you so much
It taught me to love myself
What a gift you gave me.

In loving myself
I learned that all is love
When hurt people hurt people
Remember wounds can be sourced
To let in the light.

Broken places caused by broken people
Bring more than was intended
Divine ways are not of man's thinking
Experiences given to show the way
To the better self within.

Be made supernatural
Survive, thrive, and stay beautiful
Let your heart hear that small voice
Singing your soul's song
As it remembers Itself.
A full Hallelujah
Amen

HEALING GAME

Here we are in the healing game of
Blessed divine love
The ultimate trinity of God, you, and me alone
Yet not a closed circle
Somehow all is present where the
Oneness of love abides.

Drinking the wine of love
Most rare while available to all who choose.
Drunk on the healing power of Divine
Medicine flowing through our veins
In rhythm with the Universal heartbeat.

Love with the power to rent a thousand veils:
Cultural teachings and learned behaviors
Old habits and fears
That separate us from our true selves
Each other and God.

In your presence I find divine
flashes of the map to the
Way home to self and heaven.
In your presence I feel the force
That empowers the movement of universes
The same force that
breathes us and the trees
Divine memory never mistaking the task of
Unfolding the rose while folding the cabbage.

HOW DO YOU DO THAT?

How do you do that?
One look and
I remember myself as
Divine Love as love is what we are
That same light that lights the universe.
We are made of this
Appearances and memories
Are refreshed in every cell as
The vibrations of Divine Energy
Refreshing every thought
Making known that all is well
I am that light I see in your eyes
You are the light in mine.

A negative and a positive charge
Sparks of electromagnetic energy
Available for creation
Speak what you desire
In full knowledge that
We have not because we ask not
Our time is now
We have done the work of
Learning that we are love

The promised God-Man
Reborn in Grace and Spirit Divine
Earth has waited for this birth
A gift long in coming
To green and raise up
A generation of like-minded lovers.
Lovers capable of fulfilling
The command to love one another
As God still loves us.

BEAUTY'S SECRET

Watching the caterpillar
The one who understands
The challenges and work required to
Uncover the Divine Self.
Watching you and seeing the unfolding
I have seen in myself
Alerts me to the beauty
I know you, too, will soon become.

Painful and fearful of complete loss of
Known worm-ego self
Suspecting there is something better
While melting cells change shape
Wings now undeveloped
One day will unfold
Displaying a beauty, vibrant, and strong
Now unimaginable to the unfolded self.

Born again after death has its way
Man should pay attention to the promise
Of the possibilities that abound.
Discover jewels within
Hidden yet knowable by Grace
A self waiting for its Divine Self
To be born, known, and loved.

BLOOMING

Love has awakend
The voices within me
As well as other
Gifts too much and too long asleep.
With the pen my only tool
I tell you of love's movement within.

Like sap in Spring to maple tree or
Tulips peeping through snow
The source of heat that enlivens
Unseen by naked eye
Divine energy in all things
Making itself known.

Expect to bloom and heal
Create and be resourceful.
Beauty which is love
Manna for living and giving.

We all came bringing gifts,
A command to love and
A need for each other.
Set the heavenly table.
Feast from Divine Bounty.

How easy to forget and
Allow oneself to become frozen.
A winter within.
Water that we are,
With the heat of love and passion
Let's make steam
To power, renew, and invigorate life.

BORN AGAIN AS LOVER

Life at a higher dimension
Born again as a lover
When yes is the answer.

No contractual or quid pro quo
Transactions on demand
Only the heart-informed actions
Of lover and beloved.

New ways of living and creating
With Divine spark observable in all things
Work is finished and
You've done as commanded
Learned to love
Now to live in the promised
Life in heaven on earth
Home with the oneness of love

EAT THIS IN REMEMBRANCE OF ME

As Christ said eat this bread
In remembrance of me
Thereby restoring wholeness as they had
Killed the part of self that is love
In their inability to love.

Without complete self-acceptance
We reject the self in others
The desire to kill and consume in some way
Seems to be the way to own and incorporate

So you came for my life to destroy my spirit
The ancestors tell me the Rock cleft for me
And they hid me in the Rock and administered
To me with the angels

Attempts from those who thought they owned me
And betrayal by those who said they loved me
Efforts to kill my Spirit
Yet I AM still love and still loving.

I AM LOVE

That pain I thought would endure forever
It had lingered unabated for so long
Has melted like a snowball in the
Summer heat at the equator.
It has been replaced with joy
At the sound and vibrations, I love you.
Words I repeat to myself often.

I've learned a new language
It certainly was not my native tongue
New words new thoughts new way of living
A new way of being a new way of
Seeing the world and everything in it.
Beauty appears in places and ways
Previously dull and dim.
The world newly remade in wonders
I never knew existed
Magic colors appear where
Previously dull hues dominated.

I will follow to.the end of each rainbow
Sure to find new treasures and adventures
Waiting just for.me ready to be explored
I will ask for what I want and take.nothing less
I've learned who I AM
And the magic in that knowing

I AM LOVE. I LOVE YOU,TOO.

I AM NOT AFRAID

I've been put through hell
And came out the other side brand new
Refreshed after drougt burned off
Green and growing, blooming, and sprouting.
Loved the devil, danced with the devil
As he hated and mistreated
I'm still love and loved
Covered in the Armor of God

I know who I am
That lets me know who you are
Yet I feel no need to name or call you out
What you think or do you must own
You owe me no accountability
Answer only to yourself

I'm not afraid
I've paid my dues
Found light after darkness
Don't tell me lies
My soul is a built-in detector off the ungodly
If it's not love don't come near

I SEE YOU

I know the many things you are doing
You do them all so well
I see your spirit of wanting to
Be present to all the demands on you
The power of your love is amazing.

I ask you only to be who you are
I am just loving the feeling
Loving you gives me.
Just loving how I see myself
Mirrored in your eyes.
A look that says you are
Love personified love yourself.

I reach deep into the place inside
Where all I need is stored and sourced
From Divine Spirit within
It was there all the time
Estranged by experiences and pain
Home to self and happy place
Thank for taking me there with your love.

I give the love back to you
Magnified by Divine Spirit
Which enables, amplifies, and blesses
All who share in spirit
Making burdens of earthly living lighter.

IN AWE OF THE ENERGY THAT
MOVES BETWEEN US

In awe of the energy that moves between us
Bringing us together then pushing us apart
Making known our sameness
Revealing our differences.

Like waves cresting the shore
Rushing back to sea
Movement with rest
As designed to be.

We are embracing life as it seems to be
Movement between pain and joy enough
Keep us reaching for each other
Learning how to Be.

A GIFT OF GRACE

Chosen to love another beyond
The culturally approved limits
Evidence of having been special made
To expand the awareness of
All mankind in time.
You are God's blueprint
The coming epoch requires
Exactly how you were made
And what you were made for
Not easy but you can and are doing it.

The rewards are great and the trials plentiful.
The joy of finding and claiming
Parts of ourselves and God-given gifts
Makes life so worth living even with the pain.
Every path to Self unique to each
Finding like-minded souls who
Vibrate at the same level
A pearl of great value
A joy for living.

Reveal yourself in the protective
Unconditional love we share
Knowing your self now share with me
As we both glow in
The awareness of the Divine love
We know each other to be
Fully seen, no fear, no shame, no judgement
Surrendered, whole, alive.

KNOWLEDGE FOR LIVING

The day the teacher knew it was time
To go back school
The day it became clear
That the academic curriculum
Never covered the subjects with
The knowledge most suited to
Living the life love calls one to.
That is the day education began in full.

Everything is energy and ever in motion.
Change is the only constant.
The demand for knowledge of self
More in demand in a life
Than knowing statical formulas.
How to know the love of self
So that love of others shows
That there is no other but

LOVING FEELING

I love the feeling my loving you gives
Every fiber of my being is
Wired with electric magnetic energy
I want everyone to know this love
As it has power to move self-love
To universal peace joy and new life

OLD OAK TREE

Harboring the history
Of seasons past,
Answering none of the questions
Foolish men ask.

Growing young and beautiful
When each Spring is new,
Turning gold and gray
When each Summer is through.

Nurturing all who come to you
Squirrels, birds, children, and old men, too
Rejecting none nor clinging to one
Oh! If I could be as you, old Oak Tree.

REMEMBERING THE WAY

Just as the smallest stream
Remembers its way to the sea
I am at home
Even as I flow back to you.

While dreaming this illusion called Life
Sometimes in joy sometimes in pain
Living deeply from the path you prepared for me
Every step in faith that you
Know what is best for me.

When this path ends
Trusting that it will find me at peace
Having done and seen
A life lived and a loving
Worthy of Grace to have love call my name.

THE WISDOM OF TREES

Who planted the first fruit tree?
How did the knowledge of our needs
Be known long before we could plant?
How we take without thought
The exchange of carbon dioxide and oxygen.
No awareness required or request made.
A miracle to be aware of and say thanks.

When rain falls we often complain
Of the ruined planned outing
Unaware of the plant's need for water
Unaware of our own need to drink water
Sleepwalking through Paradise
Complaining about unseen
Miracles and mercies.

Leaves don't fall off trees.
The tree emits a chemical then
Leaves are pushed off by the tree
So that it can survive winter's ice storm
To leaf and flower another Spring
In support of life's need of oxygen.
Wake up! We are missing miracles
Carrying false ideas of our own making
While waiting for preconceived
Ideas of miracles.

A poet wrote of falliing leaves
"To die is to travel a little"
I say,"To travel is to die a little"
Returning renewed to self.
Self love was always the destination.
In Self unity abides, there is no separation
May we leave false ideas and then
May we find our way home.

THIS GIFT

This gift of love that has blessed my life
And restored and anchored me to
My love of self
Is far too precious to keep to myself
Too powerful to be stored away
A Grace much too Divine for selfish needs
I must give it to the world.

Imagine a world alive with
The vibrations and colors
Our love contains
Wake up everybody
Know what is available to you .
Re-member yourselves
You too are the beautiful Joseph
The child of the King
More glorious than all creation.

Bring your battered and tired body
To the spring and drink
A living love
Share a promise restored
Thanksgiving with meaning
A Christmas of rebirths

MARRIAGE AT ITS BEST

Marriage at its best
Is an umbrella for two yet
A love wide enough
To cover family friends community
And even support and underpin nations.
So lovely to stand with you both
Under the umbrella of your love.

To find a love to share for a lifetime
Is a blessed gift worthy of daily celebration
And thanksgiving in deep gratitude.
Someone to share dreams, sorrows, gains, losses, and all that comes with living.
Joys doubled burdens lightened.

Count yourself among the blessed
And a living example of the
Power of love to last and
To grow deeper and richer
Through the years and
With all the seasons of life.
We salute you and celebrate you here
On this 40th year of your journey together.
May you enjoy many more
loving deeper still.

GOLDEN GIFT

All I ever needed is within myself
Yet it remained partially
Seen and under-utilized
Until that moment you mirrored
The treasure trove of Divine Light and
I saw my own beauty and
Saw myself as Divine love.

Thank you for being that mirror
Reflecting myself to myself.
With that generous gift
I'm free to walk away blessed.
Divine mirroring is two-way
And you have seen your own Divinity
Your beautiful soul-self.

I wait as you manifest into being
All your heart's desires
Now that you have the
Power of realized Divine Self
To actualize your purpose
And move into Life
Using the gifts you came here to give.

A PRAYER

May we all be sure
That all is in Divine Order.
We are loved, capable,
And worthy,
With no need to prove
Anything.

May we be granted the Grace
And strength and resources
To be present and available
For all whom God has placed in our care,
Especially ourselves, thereby
Enabling by example.

Deep gratitude for the gift of life,
The ability to love and share
And for the Grace that powers it all
Alive within us.

AFFLICTION OR BLESSING

Let your affliction be the key to your
Healing and blessing.
Sit in love
Come off the busy road
Look deeply within.

Acknowledge the veils that
Hide a truer self love
Rent them and reclaim
Your birthright with the help of
Divine grace so generously given.

A space where love abides,
And fear and all that does not belong flees.
Know self at one with God
And all creation in full bloom.
All needs met and sustained.

THE SILLINESS OF LOVE POEMS

Self-proclaimed wise men say that
People in love should not
Write love poems.

They will prove themselves
Absolutely silly to the culturally sane-thinking
Who carry forth right-thinking
Only those with eyes and ears
Of the heart could possibly
Understand the message the lover
Is attempting to share
It helps to have experienced
That divine gift of Love.

So why do poets keep
Writing about the inner experience?
They simply can't help themselves
A cloud can not hold the rain
when it is ready to fall
Nor can we teach anyone to love
A gift of Grace available to all.

A child can not stay in
The womb when gestation is over.
The lover has love oozing from every pore.
That light in the eye
Unmistakable Bliss we all know and want.

CHOICELESS CHOICES

I didn't write this contract
I see you didn't write it either
I see the signature is Divine.
This is a choiceless choice-making
Demands that must be honored.
Even if currently beyond our understanding
Love so out of ordinary
Demanding complete trust
Ego surrender and relaxing
Into the full knowledge of the oneness
Of the perfected Divine Love.

The fight to resist the
Release of known self for higher self
A struggle of Dark Nights of soul
We must endure.
The reward being the
Restoration of God Self
Able to live heaven on earth.
Self-love enabling love for all.

If this becomes unbearable
Go into the inner room
Close the door and scream
Fall on your knees
Look up and pray
You will probably hear the reply
Grin and bear it
It's all done for you
The better man being born.

A SAFE PLACE

To find a safe place
To practice being one's authentic self, unfiltered.
No lies, pretense, or half-truths,
Only love, total acceptance, and trust.
Being the self that God intended
And created one to Be.
A miracle for oneself and the world
A thing of beauty. Whole.

Imagine no societal scripted roles,
No box to live in or
Assigned duties to perform
Only acts performed
from heart and love.
Living from Soul, an original
Infused with spirit of Divine
Freedom in all its gifts and creativity.
A flower of rare Divinity alive and
Filled with joy radiating
As Glory on display.
A template of possible life showing
The way forward to joy for self and others.
Abundance in all areas of life.

Well, that safe place has embraced me.
I have no choice but to Become
The Divine Love I was born to be,
The surrendered life bringing relief
Sprinkled with joy of knowing after
Ego death and dark nights of the soul.
However, it's the only way through
But filled with all that's needed
For the journey to Self,
The journey to God within
Now ready to fulfill Divine purpose.

SOME MEN MAKE GOOD LOVERS

Some men make good lovers
Some men make good friends
Blessed is the woman who finds
Both in one
Blessed more is the woman who finds
One and one

MY LOVE

When I looked into your eyes
Seeing my self reflected as pure love
Is the day doubt ended and
I Iearned who I AM
And the gift of grace we all share
As God within.

We are told that we must love ourselves
Before we can love others
May be true but offers no accountability
As to how one is to learn to
Love as God loves us in our fullness
Leaving a culture which confuses love and lust.

With the knowledge of self and Source
All things become possible as promised
We came here to express our fullness as
All that love Divine expresses
Joy, peace, love, and abundance
In supply that supports life divine.

Eyes that mirror each other as God
As Love's agents one to another
The command to love each other
Well within the ability of each of us
The building blocks of the
Beloved Community in the
Restored Garden of Eden
A resurrection and new birth.

WHILE YOU ARE NOW TWICE IN THE MIND OF GOD

While you are now twice in the mind of God
Having spent a few years with us earthbound
We remember and talk of you in loving tones.
How happy we are that you joined us however briefly your stay.
You taught us much about love and joy.

How wonderfully well you completed our family
With your playful ways and engaging mind
That keen sense of humor and wisdom beyond your years.
Your absence leaves a hole in my heart nothing can fill
But I know the pain you felt for my pain
And knowing you would demand
I continue to love and enables me to keep moving.

I feel you near always as I am but a breath away
Meanwhile there are on the other side loved ones you
Knew and shared time with while earth-bounded
I know what you would require of me and I will do it
The only joy in this will be in deep gratitude
That you came to us at all
And for what you taught me about love and life.
Deep gratitude and Bon Voyage
I love you so much.